ALSO BY JOSHUA BENNETT

POETRY

The Sobbing School

Owed

NONFICTION

Being Property Once Myself:
Blackness and the End of Man

Spoken Word: A Cultural History

The
Study
of
Human
Life

JOSHUA
BENNETT

PENGUIN POETS

PENGUIN BOOKS
An imprint of Penguin Random House LLC
penguinrandomhouse.com

LIBRARY OF CONGRESS CATALOGING-IN-PUBLICATION DATA
Names: Bennett, Joshua (Poet), author.
Title: The study of human life / Joshua Bennett.
Description: [New York] : Penguin Books, [2022] |
Series: Penguin poets Identifiers: LCCN 2022006597 |
ISBN 9780143136828 (trade paperback) |
ISBN 9780525508328 (ebook)
Subjects: LCGFT: Novels. | Poetry.
Classification: LCC PS3602.E664483 S78 2022 |
DDC 813/.6—dc23/eng/20220224
LC record available at https://lccn.loc.gov/2022006597

Printed in the United States of America
2nd Printing

Set in Goudy Old Style MT Pro
Designed by Alexis Farabaugh

for my family

Acknowledgments

Sincerest thanks to the following journals for publishing earlier versions of the work featured in this collection:

Academy of American Poets: "Dad Poem (Ultrasound #2)"

Colorado Review: "Dad Poem (We play Cam'Ron at eleven)" and "Trash (The Knicks were trash)"

The Kenyon Review: "Trash (All the men I loved were dead)"

Poetry: "The Book of Mycah"

Poetry Daily: "Trash (All the men I loved were dead)"

Puerto del Sol: "Trash (Saturdays, it was my job to pick the bones)"

The Southern Review: "Trash (Abolition)," "Trash (I bought a house by the trees)," and "Trash (The American Negro is an invention)"

The Wall Street Journal: "Dad Poem (No visitors allowed)"

The Yale Review: "Dad Poem (The New Temporality)" and "Dad Poem (Your doula's name is Perpetual)"

Thank you to the family that raised me: my late grandmother, Charlotte Elizabeth Ballard; my aunts and uncles; my big sister; and my mother and father, who taught me that strength was inextricably tied to gentleness. That poems, like all good things, were meant to be shared.

Thank you to my editor, Paul Slovak, for his keen eye and willingness to try something new with me every time we put one of these together. Thank you to my Langston's Legacy family for workshopping several of the poems in this manuscript in their earliest forms: Andrea Bossi, Danielle Georges, Florence Ladd, Gavin Moses, and Patrick Sylvain. Thank you to my friends, mentors, colleagues, and collaborators, for your calls, your work, your camaraderie and laughter, especially during these harrowing last couple of years: Thomas Alston, Charlotte Bacon, Jamil Baldwin, Cory Benjamin, Everett Aaron Benjamin, Kyle Brooks, Jamall Calloway, Devin Chamberlain, Daniel Claro, Ben Crossan, Tongo Eisen-Martin, Mary C. Fuller, Aracelis Girmay, Jarvis Givens, Bill Gleason, Carlos Andrés Gómez, Terrance Hayes, R.A. Judy, Susan Lambe-Sariñana, Carvens Lissaint, Jesse McCarthy, Roshad Meeks, Ernie Mitchell, Wesley Morris, Timothy Pantoja, Gregory Pardlo, Imani Perry, Samora Pinderhughes, Elaine Scarry, Christina Sharpe, Tracy K. Smith, Josef Sorett, Matthew Spellberg, Brandon Terry, Daniella Toosie-Watson, and Simone White.

Thank you to the Whiting Foundation, the John Simon Guggenheim Memorial Foundation, the Society of Fellows at Harvard University, and the Department of English and Creative Writing at Dartmouth College for the various forms of institutional support that helped make this manuscript possible.

And thank you to my wife and son, Pam and August Galileo: You are my life. Thank you for making each day miraculous.

Contents

How do you provide for the Study of Human Life?

—June Jordan

Where life is precious, life is precious.

—Ruth Wilson Gilmore

Trash

What critics throw away I love the more;
I love to stoop and look among the weeds,
To find a flower I never knew before

—JOHN CLARE

One man's waste is another man's soap
Son's fan base know the brother man's dope

—MF DOOM

I knew life
Started from where I stood in the dark,
Looking out into the light,
& that sometimes I could see

Everything through nothing.

—YUSEF KOMUNYAKAA

I

All the men I loved were dead
-beats by birthright or so the legend

went. The ledger said three
out of every four of us were

destined for a cell or lead
shells flitting like comets

through our heads. As a boy,
my mother made me write

& sign contracts to express
the worthlessness of a man's

word. *Just like your father,*
she said, whenever I would lie,

or otherwise warp the historical
record to get my way. Even then,

I knew the link between me
& the old man was pure

negation, bad habits, some awful
hyphen filled with blood. I have half

my father's face & not a measure of his flair
for the dramatic. Never once

have I prayed & had another man's wife
wail in return. Both burden & blessing alike,

it seemed, this beauty he carried
like a dead doe. No one called him Father

of the Year. But come wintertime, he would wash
& cocoa butter us until our curls shone like lodestone,

bodies wrapped in three layers
of cloth just to keep December's iron

bite at bay. And who would have thought
to thank him then? Or else turn

& expunge the record, given all we know
now of war & its unquantifiable cost,

the way living through everyone around you
dying kills something elemental, ancient.

At a certain point, it all comes back
to survival, is what I am saying.

There are men he killed to become
this man. The human brain is a soft

gray cage. He doesn't know what else
he can do with his hands.

II

The Knicks were trash. Head colds
at the outset of a South Bronx summer:

trash. The second hour after she is gone,
the moment the song you both used to slow

-dance through the kitchenette
to comes on, moving on: all trash.

Death is trash. Love is a robust engagement
with the trash of another.

Monthly bills of any kind are trash,
although access to gas and electricity

is not, so there is that to consider.
Blackouts are incontrovertibly

trash. Much like student loans, or the fact
that we live in a culture of debt such that one

must always be behind to make some semblance
of what our elders might have called living.

My friends often state in the midst of otherwise
loving group chat missives that life is trash, though

we all keep trying to make one for some reason
or another, and the internet says my friends are trash,

that black men and boys are trash, and it makes me think
of the high Germanic roots of *garbage*—which

is perhaps the first cousin of trash—*that part of the animal
one does not eat*, and we are sort of like that, no?

Modernity's refuse, disposable flesh
and spectacular failure, fuel and fodder,

corpses abundant as the trash
on the floor of the world.

Aging is trash. I am years past thirty now
and so any further time qualifies

as statistical anomaly,
you can't expect good

results with bad data, *trash
in, trash out*, they say,

and I'm really just searching
for better, more redemptive

language is the thing,
some version of the story

where all the characters
inside look like me and every

single one of us escapes
with our heads.

III

Saturdays, it was my job to pick the bones
from cans of fish which became the unwieldy
piles of pink flesh that, once fried, became the cakes
we ate for dinner that night, breakfast the next

day, dinner again to close the loop. Decades passed
before I saw the beast in real time, realized, like Baldwin—
who once saw his mother lift a yard of velvet, say
that is a good idea, and for months thought ideas were shocks

of black fabric—that salmon lived outside
the bounds of Foodtown shelves
we searched for deals in the early '90s,
supermarket circulars held tight

in our too-small hands, armaments
against American cost. Older now,
a literary type with insurance
to boot, I tell you this story

at our kitchen table, unsure of what
I am trying to convey, exactly.
Something about the flexible
nature of human knowledge,

perhaps: a speed course in semiotics
over poached eggs. Or maybe
some version of the same tale
I am always telling, that the wall

between the world & me
grew weaker once I left
what I loved. Children
of the poor, their small words

& smaller sense of scale.
Back then, life on Earth
was Yonkers, NY,
& my grandmother's salon.

Every leather-bound book
was a Word of God. And there I was,
an affront to history, creative, even
in my ignorance, sketching planets

in the air as my big sister sang soul outside
my bedroom window, her voice
like something ancient and winged,
pulling summer into being.

IV

(CROWN OF THORNS)

The American Negro is an invention. He innovates
& endarkens our innermost visions of the human
species. The American Negro is an intervention.
He is interdisciplinary & interstellar; intellectually
amphibious, indiscriminately savage. Indeed,
The American Negro is, on average, quite humorous,
if only indirectly. Most often he is more so akin
to automata, a kind of rudimentary artificial intelligence
in its infancy. Even still, the American Negro is, in most cases,
indefatigable. An infinite resource. His anguish, infinitesimal.
His aspirations? Indiscernible. Just imagine: an invincible
apparition. An invaluable addition to the instruments
in the shed. *The indomitable soul of the Negro is an impulse
toward abolition*, some dead man somewhere wrote
in a book that I once read. *Off with his head*, they said.

They said books were the way through the brook of fire

blackness was, so my boys & I steeped ourselves in

whatever Ivy League library shelves lent us in our late

teens, early twenties, until we sparkled proper articulate

doctor of philosophy, master's, pastor, preacher, poet, scholar

of arts & human sciences, trained by institutional schemes

geared toward certain kinds of compliance, aesthetic & other

-wise, my brothers shine brightest when the lights are on.

Politics honed by threat & adoration. Theft of language

named primary education named home training named lower

your tone *don't say that* about the ones who love you enough

to put up with such arrogance as a matter of course of course

you are martyr messiah gangster never survivor son somebody's

baby boy beyond the age of five or six you see the signs

of life you cannot ever own you know the way it is.

You know the way it was back then: futility in any direction,

we figured, unless you hooped or had bars like X or Jay,

a recording booth you could use to spin those imagined lines

of verse, urgent as the discourse of markets that would one day

dart across our screens, into poetry no one knew by that name.

Or lawyers, perhaps, since we cherished argument above all

other forms. Or preachers like my uncle, who drove a midnight

-blue Mercedes, spoke with a voice that was its own object & force,

solid as the side of a destroyer. Never let them say we were aimless.

Amidst Hennessy altars & tall tees adorned with faces of boys made

ancestors by casual misunderstandings, we cast images into the air

of lives we had only heard tell of via network TV, contraband

lyrics pulled from dial-up sessions that lasted hours before

parents came home to kick us off the line, jettison the crew

back into worlds where words had an irrevocable heft to them

& we were mortal again & anonymous no longer.

Several notches above anonymous. Ella Fitzgerald

hails from Yonkers. We shed the 2 train, kept

our debt. Middle-class intentions fail in Yonkers. I left.

Wrung my hands. Got a therapist. Medicated heads

prevail in Yonkers. Whole Foods? Does not compute.

Even our hunger is loyal. It's 1999. No Jamba Juice

or kale in Yonkers. My father is a star. Prayed the pews

to tears last week. Once, his love, it lifted me. Then

my faith in blood grew frail. In Yonkers, I bloomed:

a manageable stain. Bodies falling maim the night.

Fistfights gone off the rails. We have no sense

of scale in Yonkers. The letter flew like a ghost

in a ghost costume through the front door.

A scholarship: my last piece of mail in Yonkers.

My last piece of mail last year was a book of poems by Denis Johnson

named in honor of the artist James Hampton, who built a sculpture

from tinfoil & cardboard big enough to fill a room, which it does, even

as I write this, it looms gargantuan over its own space in the Smithsonian,

labeled in accordance with its grandeur & glamour, its luminous gold

& aluminum grammar, *The Throne of the Third Heaven of the Nations' Millennium*

General Assembly, which is the only known work of art Hampton crafted

in his 55 years on Earth, the latter part of which he labored as a janitor,

night after night, gathering metal for a masterwork he built in secret, a scene

almost Vulcanic, hammering in the silent darkness of a Washington,

D.C., garage miles away from where the work would one day stand, first

discovered by a landlord on the hunt for overdue rent, the irony of which

merits consideration elsewhere, perhaps, yet I am here, first, to celebrate

James, the tireless genius, his throne built not only, you see, from what

most would call garbage, detritus, unworthy or nothing at all, but dreams

like a second flesh no earthly weapon formed against him could kill.

General consensus in our home was candy or soda could kill us,

or else rot our constitutions in some larger, metaphysical sense.

Body & soul, to cite the old wisdom. In protest, my big sister

& I would sneak the stuff through customs whenever we could:

Swedish Fish & ginger beer, Kit Kats, Mary Janes & Malta

lining the sides of each pocket like the contraband spoils

they were, smallest joys, our solitary arms in this war against

the invisible wall our parents built to bar the world of dreams.

Now that we are older, the mystery is all but gone. We were poor.

Teeth cost. In the end, it was the same as any worthwhile

piece of ancient lore: love obscured by law, our clumsy hands

demanding heaven, forgetting the bounty in our bellies,

the miracles our mother made from Jiffy mix & cans

of greens, all the pain we never knew we never knew

held there, against our will, in the citadel of her care.

In the citadel of her care, we grew tall. Memorized verses

from the King James Bible, *the evidence of things not seen*

all around us each day. Here, I learned to separate the plane

of what I could hear & smell from the landscape our mother

traversed in visions, though it was as real to me as new weather:

cold made visible by breathing, heat so high in June a crisp

dollar for AriZona iced tea seemed to me a vast fortune.

I had never pondered the long history of credit, barter, fiat,

& trade, though I knew there was a power money claimed

over us that was almost unnameable, appeared only in phrases:

Con Edison is not our friend, she said, when I left a light on for

too long, or the well-worn classic, *but do you have McDonald's*

money? Even there, I now hear a tenderness I could not before,

her making sure I knew my true home was in another realm,

another life, beyond our temporary house by the trees.

I bought a house by the trees to feel properly integrated,

whole, to cover the gaps in my long-standing

argument with our era of metal & light.

A man of the city turned back to the woodland life

not for peace, but a meaningful portion of entropy: rabbits

sprinting in pairs across the street, half-grown deer leap

-frogging bottles of Amstel behind our community

garden, where someone's responsible parents grow

squash & snap peas to honor the vanishing

world of living things no louder than the sound

of insects whimpering in their dust-sized sorrows.

You can feel the invincible bond of everything

if you just take a minute. If when the emptiness beckons,

you can leap into the blackness of its call.

Attack, balderdash, blackness (they call from the rafters), blather
-skite, claptrap, codswallop, crap, a dollop of damns in generally
pristine prose or speech, drivel, dross, effluvia, fiddle-faddle, flap
-doodle (a personal favorite), folderol, garbage, guff, hogwash,
hokum, horsefeathers (you can almost envision Pegasus mid-flight),
humbug, imitation (not the thing itself but the accusation), jazz, junk,
kaput, lambast, loss, malarkey, mass entertainment, mass incarceration's
psychic aim (a problem isn't real if you no longer see it), muck, mush,
nonsense, nuts, oblivion, piffle, poppycock, quagmire, refuse, rubbish,
slush, tommyrot, tosh, trash (as in the everyday phenomenon but
also *talk*), twaddle, undercard (ostensibly), underdog (mentally,
you recite their harms before the fight begins), vilipend, wreckage,
excess, extra, yak, youth that cannot be used, zip, zero, easy.

Zero chance we dodge the pernicious myth of ethical excess, easy

money everywhere, without the influence of various underpaid saints,

some in places you might expect, like Mrs. Riggs in Sunday school,

who taught us Truth cut in more than one direction, said Scripture was both

law & *mythos*, stories to act out in vibrant color (costumes & all) & breath

of God to weigh in community, or Mr. Bernard, local librarian, who taught

me to navigate the stacks at ten with maps I then committed to memory, or

Ms. Simms, who wrote comments on my report card like *Joshua Bennett is a witty*

elocutionist & I had no idea what that meant, so I looked it up in the big red

Webster's beside my bed because that is what my mother made me do

whenever I was faced with the unfamiliar & the unfamiliar was everywhere

those years, on campus, when Ms. Anita swiped us into the dining hall

knowing we were broke & would be for at least two more days before

the work-study check kicked in, & thus rescued us, is what I am trying

to say to anyone who will listen, the jaws of the thresher were thrown

wide open & they were what stood, masterless, unkillable, in its way.

Some of these microscopic invertebrates shrug off temperatures
of minus 272 Celsius, one degree warmer than absolute zero.
Other species can endure powerful radiation and the vacuum of space.
In 2007, the European Space Agency sent 3,000 animals
into low Earth orbit, where the tardigrades survived
for 12 days on the outside of the capsule.

—Washington Post,
"These animals can survive
until the end
of the Earth, astrophysicists
say"

O, littlest unkillable one. Expert death-delayer, master abstractor
of imperceptible flesh. We praise your commitment
to breath. Your well-known penchant for flexing on microbiologists,
confounding those who seek to test your limits using ever more
objectionable methods: ejection into the vacuum of space, casting
your smooth, half-millimeter frame into an active volcano,
desiccation on a Sunday afternoon, when the game is on,
& so many of us are likewise made sluggish in our gait, bound
to the couch by simpler joys. *Slow-stepper*, you were called,
by men who caught first glimpse of your eight paws walking
through baubles of rain. *Water bear. Moss piglet.* All more or less
worthy mantles, but I watch you slink through the boundless
clarity of a single droplet & think your mettle ineffable, cannot shake
my admiration for the way you hold fast to that which is so swiftly torn
from all else living, what you abide in order to stay here among the flailing
& misery-stricken, the glimpse you grant into limitless persistence, tenacity
under unthinkable odds, endlessness enfleshed & given indissoluble form.

21

Endlessness enfleshed in emerald & frost & shades I couldn't

name without further study. All the common weeds are here

& flourishing: bristly oxtongue, barnyard grass, broadleaf

plantain, you know the line from Whitman, about dandelions,

which rise through winter white *as if no artifice of fashion, business,*

politics, had ever been, a reminder to return to the elemental.

I feel that now, standing here, amidst what I later learn

are not filaree or velvetleaf, which I love the look of from

my book of flowers, the sound too, the music of the weeds

is what really gets to me, purslane & lady's thumb, London rocket,

mare's tail, jungle rice, the joy of discovery evident in each honorific,

belying, of course, their social status, or the verb form, which,

like *dust*, destroys the thing it names. And what is it that marks

this distinction exactly, I ask an old friend from my years

uptown, a professional. *Competition*, he says, smiling. *Wildness*.

The professionals coming to take my blood were sent by New York
Life Insurance, a fact which brings me little solace given my first talk
with their company rep: *what would your wife & son need if you were
no longer here, if you got hit by a fire truck, for example?* Randall says, and I
am fairly sure he must be reading off of index cards or something,
some laminated sample list of preapproved apocalyptic scenarios,
anything to clarify our perpetual collective peril. Extra points if you
include metal: buses, bullets, runaway cranes, a Boeing jet crash
-landing onto your freshly paved neighborhood corner. Everyone lives.
But the smoke's invisible aftermath lasts generations. In the sole image
I have ever seen of my grandfather, he glows like a row of mansions.
I am told this effect is known as *halation.* I am only half the age he was
when my father was born. All I have inherited from him are these
fists: this country that sees only weaponry when I open them.

Happy birthday, Al Roker is how every August 20th call opens

between me & Devin for a decade, shifting only once we are old

enough for mortgages, knee pain, the same blue joke about being

here at all: black men past 25 with a harrowing percentage of brothers

we chased in childhood now in chains, graves, instead of here with us,

on the phone, or else in some gentrified bar growing old over bourbon.

I can no longer recall how the ritual was built. Something to do with

my relationship to meteorology, perhaps, as it holds many things I adore

within its frame, and feels much more like the prophecy of old than anything

you see on TV these days, unless you watch the sort of shows that Grandma

did, before she went the way of everything too beautiful for permanence.

Al Roker is a weatherman. He conveys in human speech what we cannot

pull from the sky's great gray drama. The tropical storm is over his shoulder

now, spinning, harmless only at this level of abstraction. I change into the rain

-coat that matches my favorite hat. In poems, I grow immortal. Time

gathers in my hair like a silver city seen at a distance.

for Kyle, Jamall, Wesley, and Jeremy

Seen at a distance, the future looked to be built entirely from
fists: a country that imagined only weaponry when we opened
our mouths, even at our most professional, smiling, all wildness
tamed in our hair & dress. We were endless. Unthinkable form.
Mastery was the aim. The tools familiar. We stood as our cousins
had against unnameable wars: zero tolerance, stop & frisk, kin zipped
in black bags. Weights strapped to each ankle, we learned to leap
as high as the heads of trees, rode secondhand bikes until streetlights
beckoned us back to mothers, the citadels of their care, the will
to live in us so strong no weapon formed against it had a chance,
we thought, scholarships finally in hand, leaving Yonkers, Phoenix,
Detroit, Greensboro, Oakland, anonymous no longer, immortal,
if only we could learn the difference between *the way it is* & *the way*
it looks, as it says in a book that I once read, when I was young.

V
(1968)

with lines from June Jordan & Kwame Ture

The same year they assassinate
the Man Who Was Not God,

as we are not gods though
we are many, two men

are crushed by a machine
they use each morning

to keep the streets free
of everyday debris

we amass by virtue
of being here. In that city,

Memphis, that metaphysical
ground of rhythm & blues

& a certain vision
of Black America

-nness broadly construed
depending how you play

it, two men are killed
by a garbage truck

malfunction & 1,300
rise like

an incantation
in their names. Say

them. Robert. Echol.
Here, it is important

to make clear, the men slain
are not symbols. Here,

in these lines, our brothers
are no blood sacrifice

in the service of aspirational
middle-class academics

& activists, nor the ones
who mime their deadening

speech. It was Ture who said
we are the only people in this

country who shed
blood for reforms

as a matter of course.
The black corpse

as currency traded
for what exactly

Representation, they say
Politicians, an audience

that knows only
this vision of what You are

& have been here
in this land: dead

or dancing or eloquent
on television in relaxing,

screen-tested tones.
This is always the cost.

But not here, on this white
page, today. This map

of insurgencies will instead be
cast as a thousand acts of honor

outpoured & given common
speech, signs of paper & ink

& signs of flame
& trash left on the street

as if to say, we are
not the ash

on the floor of your
dreams, we are

the detonations
& the air

they breathe
into light.

VI
(*Abolition*)

A myth can sustain
or destroy. There are two
boys. One barely born & then

thrown in a cage.
The other given to tests
& excessive obedience,

an abundance of color
sprinting through
his motorized brain.

As you have no doubt
guessed, they are brothers.
One thinks like the beating

metal heart of a passenger
train with a robbery in it.
So does the other.

This is a story about the beginning
of the present order, the way in which it fell.
It begins with a prison for children

& ends with a world without cells.
In it, there is the theft of goods
& the theft of a boy's body

& they are linked in legal
documents. They stole
the bigger brother's body

& blamed the parents,
the music, the context
which made him inhuman.

This is a story that begins
& ends in darkness & the darkness
is not the midnight

of my older brother's cell
but the volcanic ore of his eyes
as he watches me watch him

play Sega Genesis on the floor
of our father's home. The code in the blood
of our bodies a decree preceding us.

The ending already marked
on the balance sheet. Our uniquely
American story unfolding invisibly

in the open air, a saber
just above our heads, cutting
the twilight in two.

VII
(Benediction)

God bless the lightning
bolt in my little
brother's hair.
God bless our neighborhood
barber, the patience it takes
to make a man
you've just met
beautiful. God bless
every beautiful thing
called monstrous
since the dawn
of a colonizer's time.
God bless the arms
of the mother
on the cross
-town bus, the sterling silver
cross at the crux
of her collarbone, its shine
barely visible beneath
her nightshade
navy New York
Yankees hoodie.
God bless the baby boy
kept precious
in her embrace.
His wail turning

my entire row
into an opera house.
God bless the vulnerable
ones. How they call us
toward love & its infinite,
unthinkable costs.
God bless the floss.
The flash. The brash
& bare-knuckle brawl
of the South Bronx girls
who raised my mother
to grease knuckles, cut eyes,
get fly as any fugitive dream
on the lam,
on the run
from the Law
as any & all of us are
who dare to wake
& walk in this
skin & you
best believe
God blessed
this skin
The shimmer & slick
of it, the wherewithal
to bear the rage of brothers,
sisters slain & still function
each morning, still
sit at a desk, send
an email, take an order,
dream a world, some heaven
big enough for black life

to flourish, to grow God
bless the *no*, my story
is not for sale
the *no*, this body
belongs to me & the earth
alone the *see*, the thing
about souls
is they by definition
cannot be owned God
bless the beloved flesh
our refusal calls
home God bless the unkillable
interior bless the uprising
bless the rebellion bless
the overflow God
bless everything that survives
the fire

The
Book
of
Mycah

There are many heroes in the black communities
across this land; most of them aren't in our books,
as yet.

—Michael S. Harper

the project of this book is also to reopen the
utopian to more promises than have yet been
imagined and sustained.

—Lauren Berlant

PRELUDE

1

Son of Man. Son of Marvin & Tallulah. Son of Flatbush & roti &
dollar vans bolting down the avenue after six. The boy grew like a
debt, & beautified every meter of the pockmarked, jet-black asphalt
which held him aloft on days he sped from much larger men along
its skin. Godfathers & hustlers, Division I scholarship forfeiters,
alchemists, liars, lasagna connoisseurs, internet mixtape DJs & baby
mama conflict consultants, each one appearing as if from the smoke
of our collective imagination, Jordans laced, drawstrings taut, all of
them gathered one by one to race the gangly, mop-top prodigy from
the front of Superior Market to the block's endarkened terminus, the
same corner where Man Man got jumped so bad at the back end of
last summer, the neighborhood residents came to regard the place as
a kind of memorial & it was like this every other afternoon, you
know, from June through the final days leading up to the book drives
& raucous cookouts which signaled our school year's inauspicious
return. This was the manner by which Mycah Dudley first gained
his fame, dusting grown men without so much as the faintest scin-
tillation of sweat to make the performance ethical. It was damn near
unsportsmanlike. Such effortlessness. Mass cruelty in a New York
City dreamscape. The laughter of girls with hip-length, straight-back
braids & baby powder Air Force 1s making every contest an event
worth leaving the perch of your bunk bed, stepping out into the
record-breaking swelter that summer held like a trapdoor for kids
with broken box fans & no mother home for at least four more
hours to fill the quiet with discipline.

We gathered in swarms to gawk at our boy before takeoff. His flesh maroon-clad from head to foot like an homage to blood, black plastic afro pick with a fist for a handle jutting from the left side of his high-top fade, his high-top Chuck Taylors, size 12, sounding like ox hooves once he entered the groove of a good run & the distinction was basically moot at that point is what I am saying. The line between him & any other mystical creature, any worthwhile myth, any god of prey or waning life.

———

The entire block was out that night. Firecrackers packed the blackening air, their fury matched only by the exorbitance of dope boy convertibles turned mobile dancehalls by the moment's weight. Which might explain why no one quite remembers when, or how, the now-infamous brawl began. Only that Mycah was in rare form earlier that evening, having just embarrassed Mars Patterson—so named, it bears mentioning, for the chocolate bars he loved to steal & trade on the 4 train, not the red rock planet or lord of war—but was now in his everyday mode, seated on the stoop, a seer with so few words for devotees & passersby, each eventually stopped asking for his backstory, for his praise or functional wisdom, & instead were content to let him eat his veggie patty with cheese without interruption, which he did. Which he was, when the din that always accompanies someone's son's public pummeling rang out, cut through our scene lengthwise, compelled the boy, for the first time on record, to leap from the steps of the brownstone his nana died braiding hair inside of, enter the scrum, and thresh the crowd for signs of the conflict's center.

General consensus has it he was looking for his little cousin, and found him, even before the first cop car ran like a living ram through the people. Before the boys in blue sprang, a spray of navy fléchettes, from behind its doors. Before they were caught in the scuffle, released ten to twenty rounds of ammo into the crowd without warning, bullets glancing off of Cutlass doors and corner store glass built for battle, all but three or four of which entered the boy mid-stride, lifted his six-foot frame from the ground, legs still pumping. For a moment, you would almost swear he was running through the gunfire, preparing for liftoff or something, little cousin held firmly in his arms, shielded from the onslaught. *They never would have caught him if he hadn't been holding that child,* said no one, though we all thought it during the weeks following that moment we each froze, the moment his body collapsed slow as petals upon the unremarkable cement, and we stared at our champion felled by an outcome so common we don't even have a special name for it.

———

Still. No one standing ran that day. Most of us turned to face his killers, hands at our sides, determined to make them make it a massacre. But all that was before we heard Man Man let off a scream so full it rent the crowd in two, splitting the circle we had built around the boy's corpse, our human wall parting to watch each casing fall from Mycah's still-wet, dark-red sweatshirt onto the street. Hear me. I heard the gunman's greeting. Saw hollow points etch apertures into the boy's clothes. They shot Mycah Dudley, quite legally. He died that night. He rose.

THE HOUSE OF HEALING

2

Just about any ordinary, God-fearing, uptown NYC–born pedestrian off the street that walked past the House of Healing in its heyday would have said, right off the bat, that its exterior was the brightest shade of blue you could imagine. Bluer than any body of water in the world. Bluer, even, than the very Platonic ideal of water itself, or something to that effect. If you went to one of those fancy schools on the Upper West, or Upper East (or Lower East, or anywhere outside a 10-block radius of the House of Healing, really), you might have used one of what the grandmothers on the block called ten-dollar words— *aquamarine, robin's egg, lapis lazuli*—to describe it. But the front door was mundane. Crayola red. Fire-truck red. Swedish Fish, hot sauce, *pozole rojo* red. On a given Sunday morning, afternoon, or evening (for in truth its worship services transcended the bounds of all three), behind that quite ordinary red door was a crowd of parishioners as diverse as any segment of the human population in this, the most diverse borough in New York City: a diaspora of saints all gathered on one accord, their beauty at last undeniable under the 100-watt honesty of fluorescent lights. Though some called them a cult—a baseless epithet if they had ever heard one—the congregants of the House of Healing knew they were there with little more in mind than the breaking of chains and the knowledge of Almighty God. Each had heard at some point in their small, difficult lives that where the Spirit of the Lord was, there was freedom. They believed it. So they assembled here to celebrate the deepest truth they knew: that they had survived what they were not meant to survive. This fact alone demanded celebration.

Seven a.m. service was a sight to behold. A story to pass on to grandchildren and the unconverted. The church mothers were all there as soon as dawn cracked open its garish fist, decked out in their Sunday hats like nylon crowns, kaleidoscopic and shimmering. The children worshipped right alongside them, of course, speaking in tongues with eyes shut tight, hands raised in total praise to the Rock of Ages. The littlest of these was the pastor's son: 5-year-old Daniel Contreras. A boy who, 30 years to the day after Malcolm X was raised from the dead & ambulated down Lenox Avenue—much to the shock & unspeakable delight of anyone that saw him there, gunshot wounds and all, unmistakable on account of both them and his hair, which was a red no one would ever think to call ordinary, Detroit Red, Revolutionary Red, and those iconic glasses like telescopes to heaven—was in desperate need of a miracle. On this particular Sunday morning in the year of our Lord 1995, the youngest member of the Contreras clan could be found lying prostrate at the front of the House of Healing, praying for a resurrection of his own. Not for any religious leader or Black Power paragon in this case, but for his mother, who was just as holy, in Daniel's mind, as Malcolm was said to be, though she was not quite as tall or well-dressed. She ministered alongside his father every single Sunday, preaching the Word with a conviction Daniel did not yet know his father envied. Though in a healthy way, of course, and no more or less than anyone might in the presence of true oratory genius.

47

Let the people tell it, to hear Daniel's mother preach was to encounter the stuff of ancient lore, that undeniable gift which made our ancestors say *lead us there, interpret dreams, state our case to the Invisible World*. In her sermons, every image came to life. When she preached on the book for which she named her firstborn son, you could almost hear the lions charge across the den, see them circling, watch them calm before the boy walked free. No, Esther Contreras was not a politician, or celebrity. But she was a mother of three, community pillar, and beloved by all who knew her. As a girl, she was the most gifted point guard her particular section of the South Bronx had seen in a decade and that was saying something. Now, somehow, she was a 36-year-old woman in a coma. One that no one had anticipated, and no doctor had yet been able to explain.

———

So Daniel prayed. And his father preached three times that Sunday. And every single member of the House of Healing incorporated an extra moment or two of divine petition into their everyday lives on behalf of Reverend Esther, even if only for a few seconds at a time. Over half-eaten breakfast and between shifts at work. Just before placing the key into the ignition, or right at the tail end of Friday's Big Game against Hamden Hall. They knew, on a level far deeper than spoken language might unveil, that the God they served was a Physician without limits. Earthly Man might have had his prescriptions and prognoses, but the Lord had the final say. The moment they heard the news, every parishioner in that building made a silent pact to pray for the woman who had for so long carried their greatest fears and dreams on her back, approached the Divine on their behalf, brought them the only moments of laughter, or relief, they might get to feel in a given week. Of course, Pastor Mike was gifted in his own way. But Reverend Esther was their shield and shining star. She was the heart and soul of the House of Healing, and there were no comforting words to make her absence anything less than a world-historical event, a catastrophe set loose in the room of their lives. It's true. Desperate times called for elegant mysticism. To weather this most peculiar devastation, they would need new protocols, a fresh covenant. Some bridge that would not break.

———

Good morning, saints. First, Daniel and I just want to thank you from the bottom of our hearts for your continued intercession on behalf of Reverend Esther. My beloved wife. The First Lady of this church. Your love has met us in our time of need, and we are truly grateful.

A wave of Amens and Yes, Lords rises from the congregation. They are with the Man of God. And his only son. And most of all with their beloved Reverend Esther, who hurt no one, and was truly anointed among preachers and teachers of the Word. Pastor Michael leans into the microphone once more.

For we know our God is a miracle worker! And so we are believing for a full recovery. What is a doctor's diagnosis, after all, against the power of the One who spoke Heaven and Earth into existence, crafted the moon and the stars, the Milky Way, from the music of his Eternal Mind?

The congregation roars its approval. They can see the moon and stars the preacher speaks of as clearly as the hands in front of their faces. They have been lifted through the sanctuary roof and into the heavens.

How many people here know that God is a healer? A friend in a time of heartache and distress? How many here today know that mortal men have . . . their hunches and hypotheses . . . but the Author and Finisher of our faith has the final word. And that word is Victory!

They are levitating now. Suspended midair in absolute ecstasy. Tears and shouts of approval ring out across the building. No one, not even the young mothers and fathers with infants in tow, remains seated. On this morning, they will not be stingy with their praise.

So, friends, in that spirit, let us turn together, our eyes trained on eternity, to the teaching scripture for this morning. It is a familiar one. From First Corinthians 6:14:

"And God raised the Lord and will also raise us up by his power."

———

Against convention, at the end of the sermon—the best, those gathered agreed, that Reverend Michael had preached in many weeks—the congregation of the House of Healing brought a single, color photograph of Reverend Esther to the front of the sanctuary. Prayed as a congregation unified. The photo measured 24 x 36 inches, just like the old movie posters at the Alhambra Theatre before it closed down for good. The sheer size of the image only enhanced the weight of the fear and sadness they already felt, fixing the picture in their collective mind such that it would never shake loose.

———

As evening drew near and each row of pews began to empty (for even the devout cannot live on the fervency of prayer alone), Daniel remained unmoved, fastened to the spot on the sanctuary's hardwood floor where his day began, eyes still closed. Versions of the same prayer repeated over and over. *Help her. Heal her, Lord. Hear me.* Just as he had every Sunday for the past three months since Esther's unexpected collapse, Daniel's father cleaned up the sanctuary all by himself. Some of the saints had offered to help, of course. But to no avail. The man needed to be alone with his only child. And with the impenetrable grief as well, now growing like a grove inside him. There was barely enough room for the three of them behind that small blue storefront as it was.

THE UNBURIED

3

The Unburied were a thorn in Daniel's side (though he would not venture to describe them in that manner of explicitly biblical speech until the Very End), and had been since the start of his freshman year. In those halcyon days of campus living, Daniel did his best to share the Good News with anyone who would listen. Comp Lit PhDs, young mothers on their way to a second job downtown, even Marquise Stevens, a fortysomething, generally unreconstructed black man who sold camouflage pants on the corner of Broadway and 119th, an apologist for nothing in particular outside the striking, underappreciated beauty of DMX's early albums. It was rewarding work. If nothing else, it exposed Daniel to a range of curse words far greater than he ever knew existed. He wasn't entirely naive. Though his father limited his social life in ways that he found absurd (he hadn't been allowed a cell phone until fifteen, and all socializing outside the watchful eye of his father was done in secret), he knew his brand of effervescent evangelicalism wasn't for everybody. Still, there was something about interactions with members of the Unburied that always got under his skin. Their refusal of the message felt personal to him. *Why believe in a Messiah you can't see*, they would say, when there was one alive and in our midst? And in public office, no less! A supreme being on earth, with a heart for oppressed peoples all over the world.

Why doesn't he perform any miracles? Daniel would quip on days when he had eaten a full breakfast and was feeling especially spry. *Why not end world hunger? Or lift his mighty finger and turn the tanks and the guns and the missiles to dust instead of talking a big game about world peace from behind a desk? What kind of Messiah can't heal the sick, or raise the dead, or walk home with his groceries in his hands on the waves of the Hudson?* Even in his anger, Daniel knew that none of these questions were offered in good faith. Malcolm, after all, had never claimed to be the savior of, well, anything. From the time of his return in 1965—only one day, the *New York Times* reported, after his tragic assassination in the Audubon Ballroom—his message was consistent. First, he had no idea who or what had brought him back from the dead. Second, he had no recollection of any mystical experience, any visions of a paradise or else some sort of hellscape, in the time between his killing and resurrection. This truth did nothing to deter the worship of the Unburied. Why would it? The first and only resurrection in modern history had transpired in their lifetimes. A man lived, and died, and returned to the work of his first life with renewed vigor. Loved ones assured them of lives worth returning to. Jobs, marriages, board positions. But the magnetism of the Malcolm story was undeniable. There was no comparison, no competition.

———

Their founder, Craig Coleridge, was a former prodigy. A 24-year-old hotshot neurosurgeon at Harlem Hospital who was working the morning Malcolm returned. Saw the undead man take that now-famous walk down Lenox firsthand. As soon as he caught sight of the martyr turned flesh-and-blood miracle, it was said by more than ten witnesses that Coleridge fell to his knees, in a mix of gratitude and bewilderment. He had not been an avid follower of Malcolm prior to that point, but none of that mattered now. He was forever changed. Later that day, Coleridge went home and composed the document that would become the guiding manifesto of the Unburied. Its central tenets were fairly simple: The Messiah had returned in a human body not once but twice. Unlike the dominant mythos in which the Messiah must leave, or else signal the End Times by his arrival, this one was here to stay. To live among us and transform the world.

———

The true calling of all who were blessed enough to witness this miracle was to act as the hands and feet and eyes of King Malcolm in the spaces he could not enter. To be, in a sense, his flesh and blood, his influence magnified a thousand times over. It bears mentioning here that Coleridge was not the speaker Malcolm was. He was a man of science, and a gifted explainer of difficult concepts, but he didn't have the charisma to build a religious sect from the ground up. This is where his medical school classmate and best friend, Regina, came in. Whereas Coleridge was at his most comfortable, most effective, when putting ideas into writing or preaching to the already converted, Regina was a master saleswoman. She made the Gospel of Malcolm sound like the most logical—and more importantly, most beautiful—story in the world.

In the earliest days, word of the Unburied spread mostly through word of mouth across the city, but by the early '80s they were a full-fledged movement, with chapters all over the continental United States. Footage of Regina's public speeches traveled nationwide alongside Coleridge's writings, and the people flocked. They all wore horn-rimmed glasses and black suits in tribute to Malcolm, doing their best to follow the documented rhythms of his early life—to eat what he ate, read what he read, and carry out his commitment to international solidarity in the struggle for racial and economic justice. The Unburied claimed that they were not only—or even primarily—a religious organization. They were listeners, adventurers, witnesses transformed both by Malcolm's resurrection and his message during his first life. The way he spoke to and treated people. For thousands of disaffected, everyday men and women in search of meaning, the unprecedented, previously unthinkable miracle of a man rising from the dead was a jolt in the dark. It awakened them from the slumber of their pain. Assured them that they too could live radical, dignified lives without the fear of death. The grave was no longer the end of things. This life was only the beginning.

———

All this history was familiar to Daniel. Against the advice of everyone he loved, he had decided on a religious studies major (with a minor in journalism) and spent the time where he was not evangelizing, or helping Dad keep the doors of the church open, reading for Introduction to Continental Philosophy, Monsters in Medieval Literature, and Religions of the Americas. The lattermost course had an entire section on the Unburied. It likened them to all sorts of other utopian communities throughout the 20th century: Shakers, the International House of Prayer, you name it. There was something undeniable, unshakable, about the group. He wasn't sure whether it was the black suits and glasses, or else the lack of any central organizing body. It all seemed a bit too flagrant. Of course, Senator Malcolm was a marvelous orator. A man of the people. But to treat him as the Second Coming? To commit, every day, to wearing two-piece black suits and glasses that he himself no longer wore anymore, and mimicking the routines recorded in his autobiography? To Daniel, their religion felt like some strange, albeit fairly original, form of idolatry. How could you worship a deity you could follow online, or call to voice concerns about various real estate developments in your area and the way they were affecting the long-established spirit of the neighborhood?

His arguments with members of the cult were soon the stuff of local legend. On the corner of 116th and Broadway, they would stand, often two or three to Daniel's immovable one, debating scripture and the shape of the universe. *The battle is already won, my young brother* one might say, apropos, in Daniel's mind, of absolutely nothing. *What battle?* he would reply, knowing some version of the answer by heart: *The battle for the soul of America.* At this the three or so devotees would bow and shake their heads in unison, a gesture Daniel imagined them practicing for hours in a bunker somewhere before going out on these neighborhood mission trips. *Why do you all care so much about America? What about the rest of the world?* A young woman who appeared to be the leader of this small, motley crew of believers took a step closer to Daniel, adjusted her white pocket square and spoke: *All in due time, my brother. But first we must attend to our affairs here, in the land where the Messiah awakened. Then we can turn our eyes outward, that we might prepare for the wars to come.*

Satisfied with this rebuttal, the group members adjusted their glasses and walked away, secure in their victory once again. Little did they know, what began on that Harlem street corner as a more or less casual tête-à-tête between disciples of the Unburied and a devout unbeliever in King Malcolm's cause, would one day blossom into the most meaningful struggle yet between a single, living individual and this growing global movement. Within Daniel's mind echoed a single phrase, sown there during his childhood in the House of Healing: *God is not mocked.*

———

There was no trace of doubt in any member of the Unburied he had encountered over the years. They could all quote the Manifesto line by line, as if it were an ancient text or personal revelation. Could he say the same for his own faith practice, for his relationship to scripture, in the moments where classmates dishonored the Gospel, or mocked the beliefs of his family and friends to his face? Deep down, Daniel knew these questions were mainly ways to dance around the distinctly injurious truth of his own, ever-darkening relationship to the Divine.

Against the relentless hammer of elegantly organized, deftly elaborated arguments (offered by Marx, Deleuze, Adorno—the chorus kept growing), Daniel did his best to hold firm to the teachings of his home church, his family culture. But he was at an impasse. At his core, he thought of himself first and foremost *as a reader*. Before he came to think all that much about any other identity marker— race, class, religion all eventually ossifying to remind him of his place in the broader human hierarchy—he had been a little boy who loved books more than anything else. Although he could never say such a thing aloud, this was the true beauty of the life of the church: the role of poems, myth, song. The very idea that a book everyone in the building had access to, and knew at least partly by heart, was a direct line to paradise.

———

Now his first love had turned against him. And what shame he felt. Columbia's student culture, the core curriculum, even the major he had known he'd pursue since the first time he heard his father say the word *exegesis* in a sermon on the plagues of Exodus—one that of course, somehow, connected them to the writing of his lifelong hero Zora Neale Hurston, as Pastor Mike was good with that sort of thing—all seemed to undermine the sense of structure which had kept his world together since his mother left this earthly realm. Or, as the saints would say, *since she went on to glory.*

These orchestrated forces had left Daniel undeniably, irreversibly alone. To square his fists and war with the World. He could deal with the derisive laughter of his classmates. But when faced with the certainty of the Unburied, something else arose in him—a rage distinct from the doubt that had been creeping into his dreams. Whatever his purpose on Earth, it was tied to this strange, impassioned group of people. The legions of Unburied against an uptown kid named after a man in a hole in the ground, circumscribed by beasts.

The dead remain that way. This was the first real lesson he had ever learned as a child, black-clad in a funeral suit his father picked out from the clearance rack at the Marshalls on 225th Street. You know, that one right off the 1 train, across from the projects where Pastor Mike had met Daniel's mother as an aspiring college athlete, hoop dreams ruined by his genetic ceiling (he plateaued at 6-foot-3 while never developing the requisite handle to play guard at the next level). Neither his father's abiding righteousness nor his own nightly prayers could awaken the dead woman. Explanatory theories multiplied in his childhood mind. *Maybe God only brings back boys?* No solace found its way to his window. That pain, over the devout, difficult years, only grew, then hardened, into wit, rigor, hunger, rage. Daniel's greatest strength was that no one ever saw him coming. He would use this to his advantage in the fight against the Unburied. He would be the light leaping forth from the darkness in each of us, our last true defense against the false prophets of modernity. Their names reverberated through his brain. Gave music to his days. This was to be his ministry: the pursuit of the Truth in a world torn asunder by rhetoric full of beauty, but no power. No power at all.

COLERIDGE

4

There was something utopian in the way that I fell, almost axe-like, into the soft earth of those early years as a med school student on the brink of something brilliant, I was convinced, living mostly on the futon in my fifth-floor walk-up in Washington Heights, eating eggs for breakfast and some combination of whiskey and pizza for everything else, an absolute mess apart from the books, hundreds of them collected over the years, my idea of art whenever a visitor would ask when I was decorating and I would say it had simply never occurred to me that one would need much more than that, not the books but the feeling they produced, which I was chasing anyway, that sense of myself as a kind of erudite disaster site, a sad man full of reasonable things to be sad about: racism and ecological catastrophe, economic collapse, interpersonal trauma of various kinds toggling between the spectacular and the mundane, epigenetic stuff, PTSD and alcoholism, fighting grown men in public while thinking of it—*reductively*, of course—as a cultural inheritance on the one hand and on the other an act of nobility, some tie to a truer time when such things were not repressed in the name of a State monopoly on violence. Which is not what I told my friends at the time, of course. But I think about it a great deal these days. I think about including all of this in the essays I hoped to write in the time before the Manifesto. An intellectual history of emotion but through a distinctly racialized lens, as I understood this then to be both my expertise and my place in the dominant order. To discern what the drums are saying, I mean. Then relay it back with a bit of flair. In the King's English. But with the urgency of the Slave.

Allow me to rewind a bit. My name is Coleridge. You can call me Cole. I am a practicing physician (despite what the mainstream media sees fit to report) and lead minister of the Harlem, New York, chapter of the Unburied. I am a vessel through which the teachings of King Malcolm might pass without blemish or alteration. I was told that you might have some questions. About our theology, manner of dress, and present political affiliations. Our holy texts and earthly allegiances. You should feel free to ask whatever you like, but with the explicit understanding that my primary role in my capacity as lead minister for this particular branch of our now international, transgenerational organization is to cast down falsehoods, and to speak the facts of what I know with as much conviction and clarity as the One Above All will allow.

———

Most of our story you know by now. Fifty years ago, a man then known widely as El-Hajj Malik El-Shabazz was viciously gunned down by unknown assailants only blocks away from where we now stand. His body was brought to the morgue the next day and remained there through the night. The next morning, at roughly 7:25 a.m.—which I know because back then I arrived early every day for my 8:00 a.m. rotation, and had just ordered a bacon, egg, and cheese from Victoria Market—I saw the Truth. I saw the god-man amble down Lenox Avenue, wounds still fresh. It was his wounds that spoke to me. In human language, I heard his blood cry out. The call was for justice. The remembrance of this moment. Retribution.

The news of his resurrection spread out across the known world on the wings of birds. Right then, I let each and every one of my burdens down. My rotation, still only minutes away. My medical school debt. Every second of formal training telling me that what I had just seen was impossible, that it must have been the product of another night of broken sleep, a result of one of the many drugs I was taking to sustain my level of productivity. Sitting in front of my television 48 hours prior, I had seen Malcolm X murdered right in front of me. As far as I knew, his body might still be warm.

Over the years, I have been asked whether seeing him walk down the street was a Paul on the road to Damascus kind of moment, or more like Doubting Thomas seeing the wounds in Christ's hands. I tend to reply that it wasn't exactly like either of those things. There is nothing quite like seeing a stranger you saw die walk again. Casually at that, down the avenue on a Wednesday, as if on his way to buy a cup of coffee. It shifts something in you that won't ever switch back. Imagine seeing the inner workings of a complex though generally familiar organism—an oak tree, for instance—in real time. The rings, root system, atomic structure, all visible via second sight you never accessed before that moment and could not explain if you tried. That's what I saw. That's what our Manifesto was initially for. I had to capture the sensation of that moment with the same deliberate intensity that inspired it, in the spirit of the very same clarity it gave me. A clarity I have committed to ever since then, every time I am asked to describe what the Second Resurrection means for us all. So that anyone who reads the Manifesto for themselves can get a sense of what exactly it is we are dealing with here; the seriousness with which we must approach the new reality we all now share. We ought to rejoice! What other reaction is sensible in the wake of an event such as this? A true, dyed-in-the-wool man of the people, a cultural hero beyond compare, chosen by the One Above All and raised from the dead. The wounds on his body closing no more quickly than they would on any man as a sign of divine imagination.

Yes, he was our Messiah returned. But he was also one of us. He bled and he healed like us. But he did not die like us. He did not pass on the way we were told that we would. King Malcolm triumphed over death, and in doing so modeled for oppressed peoples all over the world what can happen when one is willing to give their life over to the cause of collective revolt against the forces of capitalism and global white supremacy. You may already know where I'm going with this. My message for the past several decades hasn't moved all that much. There are battles to win in the name of human freedom, human dignity, and we will win them. We have on our side a man who dueled with death, and won, and came back that we might have heaven here on Earth. No pie in the sky. No paradise later and famine where you stand. No diabetes, hypertension, heart disease, pneumonia, lung cancer, PTSD, while you work your 9-to-5 for a man who doesn't know your name, or that of the woman you love, and then you die.

———

Malcolm triumphed over *meaninglessness*. He triumphed over mourning and mammon and the worship of designer dictates. Which is precisely why members of the Unburied wear our customary uniform. It has nothing to do with some staid, classical vision of our prophetic leader, or what I once heard the cultural studies scholar Paul Gilroy refer to as Black Fascism (which we do not believe exists and will happily debate with him, on television or elsewhere, at any time he wants). The black suit is a symbol that cuts in many directions. We came dressed for a funeral. Malcolm triumphed over the grave. He did so ages ago—the man hasn't aged a day since 1965—and now we mock death with our dress. We are the collective refusal of life-negating messages projected onto us from the day we are born. The world we have built, are building, needs no justification. Our champion stands true. He makes our case as he lives and breathes.

We are not radicals in any meaningful sense. We are everyday, working people, united by the fact that we are willing to believe what we have seen with our own eyes. The savior of the world is here among us. Now that you have this information, how will you live? This is not a simple question. It is one that will demand your very life if you let it. I have committed the rest of my days to helping millions of men and women, all of whom were once strangers to me, pursue their answer. Any loss I have suffered is all for the glory of the One who sits on high and looks low, even now, to secure the future of those who love Him.

———

What else did you want to know? Anything more you would like to find out about me can be discovered through the study of my writings, which at this very moment you can purchase online via Bookshop, Amazon, and the Penguin Random House website. I'm not a big talker.

CREED OF THE RISEN

5

On the 22nd day of February in the year of our Lord 1965, the state of human reality was utterly and irreversibly transformed. Content for years at that point to confine our engagement with the Divine to relatively abstract modes of storytelling and bloodless gatherings, many of us had come to think of religion as more a part of the social fabric than anything else. We had no acquaintance with the miraculous. We knew little to nothing of once-broken bloodlines mended or generational burdens shorn, the sky broken in two that manna might reach a people in desperate need. We were men and women of science. Bankers and hygienists. Olympians. Physics professors and anthropologists, each of us wandering frantically as a doe in the dark, seeking fulfillment in those daily labors we knew would never sustain us in the long term. They were good jobs. We had good lives with obedient children and houses in New Rochelle with medals on the wall. Blue ribbons and trophies from high school track, all the trappings (and isn't that a funny word?) of success, every physical representation of a life well lived and a dogged commitment to the true and the beautiful. But on February 22nd, a world-shifting occasion took place, one that altered any feasible relation we might have to the allure of property or gold, to the shimmer of nostalgia or any lingering fear about our own impermanence. On that day, in a neighborhood many would call nothing worth mentioning and many others would call mecca, call haven or heaven or just plain ours, a rift opened in human history and the One Above All stepped through. He descended from on high in human form, cloaked in mortal envelope, that we might see His face and know His purposes for us, His beloved Unburied. The man He chose as His bodily vehicle was known by many names in his *first life on Earth. Malcolm Little, Detroit Red, Malcolm X, Minister Malcolm, El-Hajj Malik El-Shabazz. Though all of these are lovely in their own way, each its own vessel, carrying a specific version of this intrepid revolutionary through a phase of his journey, members of the Unburied do not refer to him by any of these older monikers. We call him King Malcolm, or King, among other honorifics we employ amongst ourselves. This mode of address is a direct outgrowth of our beliefs about King Malcolm, and the nature of life itself in the wake of his return, which are as follows:*

ONE: *We hold that the god-man King Malcolm—né El-Hajj Malik El-Shabazz—is the living, ageless embodiment of the One Above All: the ancient, eternal presence which makes all things work together for the good of those that love Him.*

TWO: *We hold that King Malcolm was raised from the dead by the One Above All on the day after the State-sanctioned slaughter of his first earthly vessel and imbued with all heavenly powers the Holy One contains within Himself.*

THREE: *We hold that King Malcolm has returned to the earthly realm to end all mortal suffering and bring about paradise on Earth through whatever means he may deem necessary or prudent.*

FOUR: *We hold that history is not yet finished, nor the future written in advance. We believe that the One Above All is both omniscient and open to improvisation.*

FIVE: *The world is the body of the One Above All and we labor alongside Him toward its sustenance and flourishing.*

SIX: As King Malcolm is eternal in both Heaven and Earth, having already defeated death in this life, so shall we be once we leave this mortal coil. There is no death for those who believe, and confess, and walk in his example.

SEVEN: We demand immediate release from all forms of military service. As we serve the One who has conquered death, we refuse to deal death at the behest of the present imperial order, whose performance of power is little more than barbarous masquerade.

EIGHT: We hold that all earthly hierarchies on the basis of race, class, gender, sexuality, disability, creed, nationality, complexion, and any and all other such distinctions are elaborate, long-standing perversions of the vision of the One Above All, in which every one of us are embraced as beings worthy of unconditional love.

NINE: As there is no sovereign, governing body in this mortal realm which demands our fealty now that the Son has risen and lives among us, we hold that there is no government on Earth to which we must comply or pledge our lives. We are each our own Sovereign. We are each made in the image of the One Above All, and are glistening shards of His Glory.

TEN: There is a day on the immediate horizon, no one knows the hour, in which King Malcolm will stand amongst the lords of the land, presidents and diplomats and prime ministers, and proclaim his eternal rule over this realm. There will be a Great War, and from the ashes of the old world a new order will rise and take shape to replace it. Where there was once imbalance, and the unchecked ravishing of corporate greed, there will be stability, economic justice, and a century of peace. Children will go hungry no longer. We will melt down every bullet, every spy satellite and heat-seeking missile. The cold metal skeletons of this nation's guns, warplanes, and tanks will fill our steel mills across the land. From the bones we will *build new infrastructure: tunnels and bridges, railroads, a home for every citizen.*

ELEVEN: All Things Long in Their Being to Persist. We hold that all forms of life, and nonlife, are reflections of the Beauty of our Maker and hold a portion of His spirit.

TWELVE: We believe in the resurrection of the Body.

MAN MAN

6

My name started off as a joke, is what I'm trying to say. I had a growth spurt in 6th grade and have been about the same height since then so it stuck. Big Man. Little Man. Man Man. It's doubling down on the height thing, which is corny to me. Ma says it's a pretty common nickname where she's from, but I always remind her that no one is thinking about Wilmington, North Carolina, like that in Brooklyn. A name is based on what they know or can see right in front of their face. Weakness or strength it doesn't really matter. In my favorite book of all time, Toni Morrison gives this whole list of names where everyone was called something wild: *Milkman, Hagar, Guitar, Spoonbread, Washboard, Tampa Red, Empire State, First Corinthians.* My name would barely stand out, I bet. Man Man would seem downright uninspired. But it does stick out around here, especially since anybody with any real pull aside from the gangsters is known by their government name first and foremost. Take Mycah for example. We all call him that. He's never had a whimsical nickname attached to him or been known to the masses mainly as someone's son or screwup little brother.

Nah, Mycah has always had his own thing. And I'm not just talking about the state record he would eventually grab for the 800-meter dash. Or the state record the year after that for the standard 3K once he decided to try out long-distance running his sophomore season. I'm saying that ever since he was little, and I mean *little little* like 4 or 5 years old, you would just see him zipping up and down the block, a blur of blue denim and red Chuck Taylors, all the tíos and trash collectors lined up on either side of the street, stopping their morning routine for a minute to see the boy go by. I wish I could spice up the narrative and say it was all about speed. But it was mostly the strangeness of the whole situation. *What the hell was this kid doing? Where in the world were his parents? And when was somebody going to get this boy some respectable running shoes?*

The first and last of these questions were never answered in the public record. But anyone who knew Mycah well knew the answer to the second one. Marvin and Tallulah Dudley died on March 12, 1995. I remember the exact date because it's my birthday. That year, we were all celebrating the latter occasion in Ms. McCormick's English class. My mom had purchased ice cream cake from Carvel for everybody earlier that morning, which made me something of a schoolyard celebrity for the rest of the afternoon. When we got the news, it was delivered directly to us in the form of Mycah's blood-stained Bugle Boy sweatshirt and a look on his face like he'd seen what we all now knew he'd seen. Another loved one lost to the shadow of death. That catastrophic moment so close to him his school clothes carried the trace. What we didn't know, couldn't have known, is that Mycah had sprinted all the way from the scene of the crime to the schoolroom because it was the only address he knew by heart besides his home, the East New York 2-Bedroom purchased with the royalty payments his father still collected from his one hit record back in 1985, those four blue walls he knew he would not be able to go back to now, maybe ever again, because his parents were gone, their beloved human bodies made futureless by the velocity of an oncoming vehicle, the driver so drunk he would not have been able to recite his own address if anyone had asked him.

None of those details were known to us back then, though. This information wouldn't arise until years later, mostly overheard from parents, and their friends, and dug up from the internet. There was no explanatory tale offered to ease the invisible wounds of the traumatized kid standing in the center of the classroom that day. The same one who only an hour before had been ecstatic about the fact of his parents dropping him off at school. Who would for the rest of his life despise even the thought of driving, but always in casual conversation make it about his identity *as a true New Yorker*: a stalwart champion of public transit, or something to that effect. He never really got past it. What would that have even looked like, given the way we stared at Mycah when he first barreled through the doors, more animated than we had ever seen him? Asking for Ms. McCormick to call *the amber lamps* to come help out his mom and dad, the phrase like something you might read in a fantasy novel: a fleet of floating lanterns sent off by elves to heal the sufferings of Men. But Marvin and Tallulah had each died instantly, the impact of the collision absorbed primarily by their bodies, shielding their small and only boy. Ms. McCormick escorted Mycah to the principal's office. We finished the cake quietly as a class. We were supervised by the fourth-grade art teacher, Mr. Valentino, who had seen Mycah running down the hallway and gotten nervous. I didn't see him again for almost a month after that. No one else did either. By the time he got back, the energy storm had gone from his eyes.

He was always a quiet kid. But now you couldn't get two words out of him unless you were bartering for snacks, or engaged in some other improvised form of second-grade socializing. But even that was a challenge. It would be years before I or anyone else realized that his vibrance had not left him, exactly. It had simply traveled elsewhere. Transferred to the areas of the body where it would be most useful. By the time we got to high school, Mycah was known all across the borough as one of the most talented track-and-field prospects of the past twenty years. No nickname ever stuck. There was simply no myth big enough to hold him. Mycah Dudley was enough.

MYCAH

7

What do you want to know, exactly?

How it felt? Where I went? Imagine blackness everywhere, punctuated by sparks. I was floating, fast, and then I wasn't. I was running with my cousin in my arms before I flashed out of my body for a minute. The days felt like days. I had nothing but time to think. I could remember everything I had ever seen, clearer now somehow than in the moment of initial encounter. My first bowl of Lucky Charms. Each individual grain of every rainbow and marshmallow star as if it were under a microscope. My parents' voices still audible in the background. Sunshine pouring through the window. The beams of light hitting my shoulder had their own mass.

Then the school dance. They are playing Sean Paul's "Gimme the Light" and each of us is invincible at 12 years old, singing in satin-smooth patois we don't understand. Ashley asks me to dance. I admit that I do not yet know how. She places my hands on her waist, and initiates me into the world of miracles. My first footrace. A summer filled to the brim with protest songs. I am eight and a half years old and have only had one haircut since winter. My parents do not believe in cutting it for reasons that are explicitly nonreligious. Though my father does always make reference to a man named Samson when I ask him about it. The most prominent person by that name in our house is a 7-foot-4 center for the 1980s Houston Rockets. My father has a poster of the man, this living titan, on the living room wall. I am tall just like him. Not quite 7 feet, but the only boy in my class as big as a 6th grader. I am also fast, but don't know how fast yet. Which is why when Mars asks me to race to the corner for a quarter, I think only of the candy I can buy with that kind of money, and not much at all about the odds. It's just not the way my brain works. It's an order of operations kind of thing.

The contest isn't close. Three full strides into the race and I've blown clear past Mars into the deep green of the park across from home base: my grandma's neighborhood corner. All this just in time to stop in at the corner store, claim my prize before the cheese bus comes. I thought Mars would be upset. I didn't even have a quarter to give him if I had lost. His expression was one of shock and awe above all else. *What the hell, Mikey!* Another outcome I hadn't quite clocked. Disappointment. Like I had left him out of a grand adventure. It wasn't some big secret I had kept from him. There were no secrets between us back then. Only distance. From that day forward, everything was different. Word got around school that I was the fastest kid in our grade, and this became just as important as whether another kid could do the newest dance, had all the freshest Jordan retros, or a cool older brother with a car paid off by virtue of his creativity and dogged determination alone. At recess, I ran circles around every competitor. I liked life better this way. No one could get near me.

———

By 9th grade it was an organized thing. Track team, local meets, testing my legs out against the best comp in the city. Sprinting left me empty. Once I hit the high about halfway through a given race, I could barely feel the sole of either foot. I was a single, honed muscle, electrified by the sound of the crowd, the metronome in my head ticking like a weapon. When I was caught up in the pace of the run that way, I wasn't just some tall kid with big hair and dead parents. I was something mechanical. An unstoppable force. Pure lightning. Pure light.

That night, the only thing on my mind was getting Matthias out of harm's way. The party had been pretty dry up to that point. Everyone was enjoying themselves, or seemed to be, but I couldn't get much into it. I hadn't run my best against Hopkins earlier that week, and I was exhausted. Plus Lily and I had gotten into a fight that day over something ridiculous. Texts she found in my phone. Evidence of what she said she had known for months would eventually lead up to this roaring, more or less one-sided altercation in the middle of Applebee's. That I had never really loved her. That I didn't love anyone or anything, as far as she could tell. Not Mars or Grandma, not even running, though I gave it all the time I could spare. I stared off into the distance. I remembered the last time I had let myself feel anything that cost me. I wasn't about to go there again. Not for Lily. Not with all these people staring at us, like an exhibit behind pressurized glass.

People always ask if I heard or saw the cop car first. What difference does it make? I wanted my little cousin to live. It was clear once darkness fell that things were about to get wild, so I was on edge already. Heartbroken, exhausted. Definitely not in the proper headspace to deal with a baton to the back or getting slammed against the wall and asked if I had drugs on me. Or a gun. Or whatever other instrument the cop envisioned in my hands months before we could even meet in the flesh. I keep calling Matthias my little cousin, because he is, but like me he's tall for his age. I knew when I saw the cop confront him there was no way he would believe he was only nine years old, and so I snatched him up, not wanting to interrupt the officer and set him off in any way, and that's when it happened. So quickly I thought the shots were ringing off much farther in the distance. At someone else's wayward son, out at the block party when he should've been inside studying biology, Kafka, how not to die the way his brothers or uncles did. The way they always seem to. It was the sound, then the feeling (a white-hot sharpness spinning through me), then the sight of six holes in my burgundy Champion hoodie, where there were none before. I fell to the ground. That's the last thing I remember. The lightness preceding the concrete's embrace. Then everything going quiet. Then speed.

Forget any of the Hollywood representation you've seen. My body, whatever moves through it to make me, came undone. Then snapped back into place like bone. I looked into the eyes of everyone I had ever known, the eyes of so many I had never so much as asked for their names, or directions to the 2 train back when I was still young enough that such matters were not encased in the mud-stained, bulletproof case of my memory. I was gone, and then I wasn't anymore. In the time between, the entire world shattered at its axes.

DARIUS

8

I was holding my phone when he fell. Originally, my intention had
been to make a work of improvised art from the footage of my
homegirl dancing on top of an abandoned cop car like a pop diva but
the shots broke all that up. I posted the video as soon as I got home
and the numbers went crazy from jump. Views ballooning each time
I refreshed. I wanted to scream but my abuela was sleep in the next
room and you know how that goes. I'm not trying to catch a
chancleta thrown at warp speed across the kitchen, so I chilled out.
Didn't make a sound but I texted the homies for sure. We were so
hype about the damn near instant Diamond status of the video (and
the Instagram post and tweet I threw up right after the YouTube
link) that we barely talked about the wildness of the footage itself.
Steve bet a bill it was all some big misunderstanding. Either camera
angles playing tricks or the young man had the world's best,
lightweight bulletproof vest on. Couldn't have been the cops shooting
blanks on account of the blood, you know, but he also wasn't trying
to hear off the rip that it must have been Jesus. We all believe. We
all live with our elders and overhear them praying for God to cover
the apartment with grace, like a fog that would fall evenly over even
the smallest of us. Our Lady of Mercy. Our Lady of Fearlessness
in the Face of a Brutal Regime. Keep us from stray bullets and
budget cuts. The mayor's running for president and half the kids in
our building can't eat. What does a miracle mean for people living
like that? What does it do for them? What does it do to them? I woke
up to DMs from local news outlets across the city asking to post the
video. I thought about what my big sister would say. In her honor, I
demanded every single cable news social media intern who hit me up

pay the kid in cash. $100 for the raw footage or I'm good on permissions. I cut a deal about eight different ways. Threw ads up on the YouTube video later that day. Made enough to cover groceries for the rest of the year. All it took was one teenage boy, for once, to return from the dead intact. Woundless. Without a mark from the taxpayer-purchased slugs that flung him from the Earth. If you take a second to think about it, all this chaos started with me. And no one knows my name. Not even you, dear reader. To you and millions of others now, I'm just some kid behind an anonymous YouTube account. A steady hand behind the lens in the three minutes and twenty-seven seconds it took for the history of the whole damn planet to shift. You want to know about the title? "Black Boy Comes Back From The Dead #BlackLivesMatter #BedStuy #HeRose" was the first thing that came to mind. Figured the hashtags would boost the video into all the right places. The rest speaks for itself. You never seen no video of anything like that. Not with that title, not with that (what does Mr. Simmons call it?) *narrative trajectory*. I seen a dead man before. Dead friends, cousins, all that. Seen my uncle laid up like a butchered calf in the street, knife wounds to the chest and neck. Ex-best friend caught him with his current ex-wife and it was on. I'm no stranger to the song and dance of intimacy turning into a kind of everyday violence everyone sees but no one knows how to explain outside of words that don't really fit. So I stick to the necessary nouns, verbs, and adjectives. The black boy killed comes back. Black right in front, first word up, so you know there's an urgency to it. No doubt in your mind there's danger involved. My boys ask me sometimes why I didn't go on TV or anything like that when the footage first got picked up. I told them to take two seconds and look at the life of the kid I captured on film. People follow him everywhere now. He can't step out onto the block without drawing a crowd. They think fame is a ladder. It isn't. Fame is a net. And there's no way to know what you'll catch with it. $800 for me to stand still and bear witness to the new world at its genesis. I'll take that any day. That's way more than good enough for me. That's gold, baby. That's gold.

MALCOLM

9

There are, to this point, enough accounts of the life I lived before death and the one I have set out to live with dignity since. My truest orientation has always been toward wisdom, liberation, and knowledge. Knowledge of who I am, and who our people are. Who and what we have always been. It was never my expectation that the knowledge of death might be added to the list of what I learned on this Earth and lived to tell about. Such an idea is contradictory on its face. There is no one, no one, more surprised by the matter of my return than me. As I lay there on the Audubon stage, the assailants' bullets still rotating, I made peace with my god. Whispered a prayer. Thoughts of my daughters sped across my darkening mind. I saw the killers' faces. Each of them. And to this day I have not pursued any form of retaliation, through the courts or otherwise. Every man is a composite of a certain kind. We are like stone eroded over time, every experience leaving its mark, its weathering, in the deepest parts of each of us. I bear the trace of dead ancestors and the lessons they left for me, here, in this world. Since I have returned, I have heard their voices ever more clearly. And so I do not, and never will, claim to be any kind of megaphone for the Almighty. My cause is justice. Righteousness is my only shield. My present focus is the destruction of the interlocking systems that hem us in, as well as the language that sustains them. I lost both of my parents, as many of you know. The lynch mob killed my father. The carceral state masquerading as medical care took my mother. Later on in life, the cages and chains got me as well. An inheritance and its opposite. The elaborate theft of our social wealth over time. Extraction: the black gold within us snatched, plundered, generation after generation. I saw it, as through a darkened length of glass, when I was in that cell. And a bit more on every step of my journey. And it was only as I passed not forward, or backward, but simply *through* the infinite enclosure of death that I saw another vision for myself.

———

It had nothing to do with becoming a politician, in the beginning. It was about the cost of milk and bread. The quality of water in my niece's public housing complex. Reparations. And if not the confluence of these social goods—what we are owed one half-acre plot and cash payment at a time—then it would be war. I knew this little more than a day or so after my return. My enemies knew it as well. The terror which had for centuries, reasonably, gripped any number of the millions of us currently living as denizens of this captive nation within a nation, seemed to simply fade into the background. An epoch of fear demerited by this strangest of miracles, this spirit returned, held in this imperfect, earthen vessel. With the threat of the uprising of millions as a saber in our hands, all the usual suspects came to the negotiating table. Mayors, union leaders, police chiefs. They saw our strength, at last, laid bare. For the first time I could remember in years, I did what I was asked. I ran for office. Unopposed. With a kind of vocal support that was unthinkable only one year prior.

———

Coleridge? He's the sort of man that's difficult to describe without falling into either ad hominem attacks or disparaging language unfit for the tenor and tone of this conversation. The man is a charlatan. A disaffected malcontent. A misanthrope. Known to mishandle truth whenever it's right in front of him. I do believe that he saw me that morning. But what he's made of that moment in the years since I simply cannot abide. Despite numerous requests, both in person and in writing, neither he nor any of his comrades will cease their strange imaginings. I wish I had another miracle in me. But I can no sooner heal the sick than I can make a flock of birds appear from the air above us right now. It is precisely this, precisely this lack, this inability to snap my fingers and fix what so desperately calls out for repair, that led me to this current path. We have had so many freedom fighters. And too many corpses.

———

So I chose my own ending this time.

DANIEL

10

I can speak for myself.

The pain that made me brought me here: to the convergence point of two movements, one still in its infancy, the other built over years of worship and struggle. My talk with Darius was only the start. I spent hours on the block that day, and countless more over the next two months, collecting data about that night and its ripple effects. I caught sight of the boy king himself only once. Totally by chance. No one would give me an address, or any local haunts I could stalk for clues. He was as big as they say. As quick too. The boy didn't outrun death, let them tell it. He ran *through* it, and death itself bent to his speed. I don't know much about Mycah Dudley. All I have to go on is what the good people of Brooklyn tell me, and when they do talk it's all hagiography. You would think he invented air.

———

I should say something about my mother here. If there is a hereafter, some palatial paradise, even if only for the most indisputably good among us, then she is there. First-chair clarinet in the symphony of Ages. We don't have a good category term for angels. *Chimera* doesn't quite cut it. Centaurs, satyrs, minotaurs: What do you call those forms of life? Those collisions of human and animal, blurring every border? As a kid, I thought that angels were half-bird, but that's not quite right, is it? In the Biblical account, angels are before birds in the order of creation. It's the birds that are part angel. Humans take up what remainder is left.

———

When I think of my mother's present form, whatever it may be, what breath remains in this lessening frame escapes from me. It's like what she said, when I was a boy, about why we didn't have images of God in our sanctuary. *You can't see the One Above Us, Daniel. That's the point. Imagine the best version of God you can, and carry that with you. The most tender and merciful and good.* I did until I couldn't.

I don't know how to tame the thing in us that needs what happened to the boy to be real. But there's nothing I've found in an ancient text, or the bottom of a glass, or the wonders of the natural world that reflects it with sufficient power. The good in him is the good in us. The ugliness too. You can't know, can't love, someone who lives outside of death entirely. What those people online feel is fear. They just don't know it yet. But I'll show them. Whatever the cost. Whatever comes.

———

Here's the thing about us. Our people. When we praise, we do so with an eye toward the despised. Our overcoming is ongoing. My hope is that whatever writing one day comes from this—whatever I craft as a result of everything I've ever known about the universe exploding to splinters—might contribute to what the saints uptown used to call *our tradition*. That collective of voices, beloved yet unsung, resounding across time. The cloud of witnesses giving texture to the sky. My mother's voice like another ark. An open boat overrun with marvelous light, pulling me through the blackness from which every incandescent thing is born.

Dad
Poem

The rule is love.

—SYLVIA WYNTER

I

The smartphone app tracking your growth says
you are the size of a blueberry today. Then a kidney
bean, then a grape, then a kumquat & a pea pod
in that exact order. In the earliest days, I listen
to your mother's stomach for the rumbling of what
I know is only breakfast, but imagine is you pirouetting
into Being, charging up as we prepare the apartment
for your entry. Pardon my theatrics. I'm usually
a man composed entirely of charts & graphs
on the inside, & need data points for everything,
an incontrovertible fact which makes your mother laugh,
since she's the scientist & I'm the writer, but anyways,
my blossoming baby boysenberry, there's so much to see.
We bought you a rug with the entire alphabet on it,
a onesie the color of turmeric honey. We're crafting
all manner of invisible things to keep you safe.
Including ourselves. Building new people
on top of the ones who made you to be worthy
of the goodness you hold & are. Keep going.
Little lodestar. Galaxy in miniature. World within
worlds, unfolding like an ebullient blue idea,
unmappable as the physics in a dream.

II

No visitors allowed
is what the masked woman behind
the desk says only seconds
after me & your mother
arrive for the ultrasound. *But I'm the father,*
I explain, like it means something
defensible. She looks at me as if
I've just confessed to being a minotaur
in human disguise. Repeats the line. Caught
in the space between astonishment
& rage, we hold hands a minute
or so more, imagining you a final time
before our rushed goodbye,
your mother vanishing
down the corridor
to call forth a veiled vision
of you through glowing white
machines. One she will bring
to me later on, printed & slight
-ly wrinkled at its edges,
this secondhand sight
of you almost unbearable
both for its beauty and
necessary deferral.
What can I be to you now,
smallest one, across the expanse
of category & world catastrophe,
what love persists
in a time without touch

III
(*Ultrasound #2*)

with a line from Gwendolyn Brooks

Months into the plague now,
I am disallowed
entry even into the waiting
room with Mom, escorted outside
instead by men armed
only with guns and bottles
of hand sanitizer, their entire
countenance its own American
metaphor. So the first time I see you
in full force, I am pacing maniacally
up and down the block outside,
FaceTiming the radiologist
and your mother too,
her arm angled like a cellist's
to help me see. We are dazzled
by the sight of each bone in your feet,
the pulsing black archipelago
of your heart, your fists in front
of your face like mine when I
was only just born, ten times as big
as you are now. Your great-grandmother
calls me *Tyson* the moment she sees
this pose, prefigures a boy
built for conflict, her barbarous
and metal little man. She leaves
the world only months after we learn

you are entering into it. And her mind
the year before that. In the dementia's final
days, she envisions herself as a girl
of seventeen, running through fields
of strawberries, unfettered as a king
-fisher. I watch your stance and imagine
her laughter echoing back across the ages,
you, her youngest descendant born into
freedom, our littlest burden-lifter, world
-beater, avant-garde percussionist
swinging darkness into song.

IV

A boy, I am told.
The familiar numbers fall
like a wall of ash across my mind,
the future now made
both freshly opaque
& terrifying in its clarity.
I know what I have
survived. I have lived
to tell of it only in songs
I can belt without ending
the world. But enough
of the untold terrors we know.
There is an entire genre
of poems about the fear
of bringing another
black son onto the Earth.
I refuse them all.
Little one, they are not ours
to bear. There is a war
outside, yes, and inside
our home there are books about flowers,
ten-speed bicycles, dinosaurs with names
you can't even pronounce yet.
We are building a story
for you that is bigger than bombs
or the words of assassins
who do not love us.
Your inheritance is this refusal

and infinitely more: triceratopses, hyacinth,
racing uphill in our blue
helmets, two runaway ice comets
cracking the night air open,
so swift within
its shadow
we are almost invisible.

V

We play Cam'Ron at eleven & the boy takes flight,
drums against his mother's form in lock
-step with the electric bass emanating

from my modest plastic speakers, a kind of minor thunder
-storm, enclosed in midnight's temperate embrace.
We got this house to raise him in & pack the walls with lyrics

born of financial markets all but decimated, racial capitalism, war
poetry of an era we barely remember now, mainstream radio accounts
of actual fugitives set free only in the air

between platinum chains muted by engineers
& microphones built from stolen metals,
the blood binding them & the men in the mines

blurred by American avarice, the romance
of narratives ending in home. We're all here.
My son, my wife, and I, the three of us alive

inside a Massachusetts town I discovered reading lines
from David Berman. I was 26, seated in classrooms
full of strangers who looked the way I imagine

the boy dancing as I write this does, our blackness
a bridge across every militarized zone, the music
in him so mighty it shifts the weather.

VI

Your doula's name is *Perpetual*,
which is an especially elegant word
that means some things are so good they go on
long past the might of our mortal eyes.
Our affection for you is perpetual.
Our attention, for you, is perpetual.
The modern world is not perpetual, and neither
is the Earth, though my sense is the latter
will last much longer. Another word
for perpetual is *everlasting*, and that's one
that your grandparents love, as it was ubiquitous
in hymns we sang when I was barely big enough
to lift the red leather books which held our psalms
on my own. When I could not manage believing
anymore, I read a man named Meister Eckhart. He once
wrote, *every animal is a book about* God, or something
to that effect. The scale of such love was a revelation.
Ubiquitous is an unwieldy word. It means *everywhere*.
You are a palace of books about God.
My love for you is ubiquitous. It shines in the eyes
of trees outside our kitchen window,
beetles giving color to the front yard,
every single brick in the room of your life
we are building, even now, as we dream.

VII

The fear a father feels
is not remarkable
only for or in its intensity
is a sentence
I want to say to no one
in particular, though
I really do mean it.
Clearly, there is a kind
of ultimate vulnerability
built into the spatial
dynamics of this whole
watching another life speed into actuality
process and dance. Your mother
drives herself to the grocery store
and suddenly you are both there,
in the grocery store, in a world
where everything ridiculous
happens beyond the control
of any one of us, least of all,
perhaps, your father,
who is sitting on the couch
right now, trying to craft a lecture
on 20th century poems centered
around public gathering,
since we can't really do that
anymore, and it felt like the best thing
he could contribute to the historical
moment. It's Thursday. In the spot

where I'm writing I'm thinking
about the worst things
anyone ever said
to me or your uncles, Grandpa,
for no reason other
than meanings they map
the moment we enter the frame.
No prelude. No conflict
or probable cause.
And I actually, openly,
weep, son. In front
of Mom. *I don't want*
people to treat him like that,
I say, entirely in earnest, as if
I am the first person
to have the idea.
There is nothing
I would not do
to shield you.
My trepidation is nothing
if not an introduction
to a new and previously unthinkable vision
of myself. A starship destroyer
in orbit; orchards atop ashes;
a castle of falcons lifting you up
and through the available expanse,
your laughter like the arguments
of angels, giving texture
to the atmosphere.

VIII

(A Storm, a Chase, Your Big Day)

Mom wakes at four a.m. to clarify
you're on the way, for real this time,
and that there's no need for stress

on my part, although there is actual lightning
woven through the black expanse outside,
tessellations of rain thickening the opaque air,

hospital bags we assembled to prepare
for this day resting like investments
at the bottom of the stairwell, our reason

-ably priced Toyota perched out front to carry us
to your grand debut. Who, exactly, is this
version of the man who will raise you,

whose first words once he hears
the news are, *Wow! Are you okay?*
Do you want me to make breakfast?

I sound, I think to myself but do not say,
like your grandfather. Toast & eggs at day
-break were his best thing. Dawn

opened its boundless jacket,
& the man fell into action
instantly, the first sounds filling

our home each morning
the sizzle of salted butter & early '70s
Stevie Wonder, like an older brother

shaking me awake. So it's me & Mom
& spinach omelets to start the day.
The Office reruns in the background

to temper stress. I can't sleep. Haven't all week.
And by the time you announce yourself again,
I know we are up against more than just

the weather. I pack the car, quick as a cartoon
hero in hot pursuit. Speed down I-95
toward Cambridge, the same town

that raised your mother, called me here
at seventeen for a two-day college visit
with freshmen named *Killa* & X, fresh

off the SATs, anxious to discern the shape
of the future. Ten years later I'm back again,
an amateur wheelman weaving

through the wake of a storm almost
as loud as the music in my mind, helping me
keep the beat of highways practiced with Mr. Lee,

my driving coach, weeks in advance. *More power,*
he would yell, like a more radical rendition
of my own consciousness, calling in

from another life. We reach the clinic
for COVID tests just in time. Mom describes
hers as *worse than being punched in the face.*

Grandma's apartment is right around the corner. We decide
to labor at her place. We dance & breathe. We watch
Steve Harvey give away thousands of dollars

for solid guesses at public sentiment on daytime TV.
The hours pass slow as the transformation of stones.
Until they don't. When it's time, Mom knows.

No one at the hospital picks up the phone.
The building elevator is impossibly slow.
We walk until we can't anymore.

Our family car is still four
blocks away when your Auntie
Alexa devises a plan.

She will keep things calm
until I can scoop you all up,
dash through back streets to get us

to the hospital lobby, yoga breaths
punctuating every three minutes
between Mom's righteous critiques

of my driving skills, ratcheted up
to eleven. We arrive. Slide
from the car as carefully

as we can. *She's in labor!*
I yell, and care workers lift us
ten flights in an instant.

For forty-two hours,
Mom wars at the limits
of human vigor, pushing

& swaying, breathing like a boxer.
You soar through the doors
of Being, terrifyingly

quiet at first, then booming,
supersonic, an ecological event.
I hold you to my chest.

Your eyes are yet
unopened. You test
out your lungs again

for good measure, filling the room
with your entirely unprecedented
music as midnight flexes its wings.

IX

The god swimming in the greenness
of those trees is the same luminous smoke
that lives inside this lumbering husk,
I think, and almost say, to the boy
in my arms this morning, the totality
of outer space displayed in a one-act
play on his cotton pajamas.
He will inherit this place.
Even the hammock & driveway
hoop. The backyard where we now sway,
its grass the color of his mother's
sweater on our first date, iridescent,
bright as venom. We are here
to listen to the song of what
does not speak, but is older
than language, and more muscular.
Where symbols end, and there
is only the overheard altercations
of birds, who taught us song centuries
ago, who cast their migratory dance
like a living painting across the wet air
just before rest. Three or four alight
on the branches of the oaks towering
above us now. Whose invisible wisdom
is everblooming. Who stand guard,
without fanfare, as I write
the first lines in my mind.

X

You can't have apples with everything,
we say to our son over breakfast, but that's
not technically true. He knows this, I suspect,
though his face reflects a certain understanding,
as if he's willing to negotiate. Before we moved here,
I knew so little of apples, their untamed array
of shapes & names: Ginger Gold, Honeycrisp, Crisp
-in, Cortland, Cameo. Both Rome & Empire,
somehow, which feels like it must be an inside joke
between members of the committee. Fuji, Winesap. Ruby
-Frost, which could be either a miracle or a plague,
I can't decide which. Paula Red is a Soviet secret
agent. Envy is a deadly sin. Holstein & Ambrosia
have skin like a storm on a televised map. On the ride
upstate to the orchard, I recount all the types to myself
in a private game. Select my prize in advance. Bags filled
with Liberty & Jazz will be my aims, like any good
American. Two months earlier, it is not yet my birthday.
I am in an office in Brighton. The doctor has never seen
a case quite like mine. During the tests, I make every task
a language game, even the ones with semicircles & blocks.
This part of my mind is *hypercharged*, he says, like a quasar,
or loving dispute. That morning, I cut a Braeburn into eighths
and cast the pieces into a small blue bowl: a handful of rowboats
swaying. At the orchard, we are stars set loose across the mind
of a boy in a field on his back, dreaming with both eyes open.
We run for hours. We gather enough apples to sate ourselves

for weeks on nothing but their cold red wealth. What marvels:
this most metaphorical of fruits, Newtonian, Edenic, pure
delight. Mighty & bright. And the orchard like a coliseum
of planets you could hold in your hand.

XI

The boy taps me twice on the chest & that means *go*,
the way it does when you're talking to a horse.
The tree felled by the storm by the side of the road
on our family walk, its chestnut branches posed like antennae

singing silently into the charismatic sky, is also a horse. A poem
is where the language of the material world collides
with the divine. The poem rides the human mind
like a horse. The boy sees the red station wagon outside

the window and says *car*. Points to my watch
and says *car*. Aristotle says to be a master
of metaphor *is the one thing that cannot be learned
from others, and it is also a sign of genius.* No one

I know ever says their kid is a genius, aside
from the boy's mother, who is the best of all
worlds. Is *car*, in this instance, a metaphor
for movement or machines? Today, I am flying

to Virginia to help my uncle leave the Earth.
In the plan I have devised, I will show him
a digital photograph, say *this is my son*, knowing
the image cannot adequately reflect his splendor

nor his complexity. Growing older means
I am more acquainted with speechlessness
than ever before. I press my hand to the tree
in the backyard and say *tree*. The boy

is quiet. Rests his head against my own.
The tree says nothing I can translate
without prayer. There is a place the poems
cannot travel. Now, I live there.

XII

(The New Temporality)

No poems, not even
one, since the minute
you were born. Now, I live
the thing that was the writing,
more intensely, alongside you
each day. Hours blur,
and are measured
only in feedings, naps
just quick enough to not subtract
from your later dreaming.
Mom & I divide the night
into shifts, dance through the fog
of sleep deficits doctors say
we won't feel the weight of
until wintertime. So what.
Our home glows
like a field of rushes,
moonlight ensnared
in their flaxen heads.
Most early mornings
with you are mine.
We play the elevator
game and improvise
lyrics, rhyming *August*
with *raucous, florist, flawless.*
As I write this, you rest
in a graphite-gray carrier

on my chest, your thinking adorned
with language that obeys no order
my calcified mind can
express. Tomorrow, I will
do the thing where I make my voice
sound like a trombone, and I hope
you like it as much as you did
today. There is no sorrow
I can easily recall. I have
consecrated my life.

AUTHOR PHOTO BY KATHY RYAN

Poet, performer, and scholar Joshua Bennett is the author of two collections of poetry, *Owed* and *The Sobbing School*, as well as a book of criticism, *Being Property Once Myself: Blackness and the End of Man*. His first work of narrative nonfiction, *Spoken Word: A Cultural History*, is forthcoming from Knopf. He received his PhD in English from Princeton University, and is currently a professor of English and Creative Writing at Dartmouth College. His writing has been published in *The New York Times Magazine*, *The Paris Review*, *Poetry*, *The Yale Review*, and elsewhere. In 2021, he was the recipient of a Guggenheim Fellowship and a Whiting Award in Poetry and Nonfiction. He lives in Boston.

GAROUS
ABDOLMALEKIAN
Lean Against This Late Hour

PAIGE ACKERSON-KIELY
Dolefully, A Rampart Stands

JOHN ASHBERY
Selected Poems
Self-Portrait in a Convex
  Mirror

PAUL BEATTY
Joker, Joker, Deuce

ZEINA HASHEM BECK
O

JOSHUA BENNETT
Owed
The Sobbing School
The Study of Human Life

TED BERRIGAN
The Sonnets

LAUREN BERRY
The Lifting Dress

JOE BONOMO
Installations

PHILIP BOOTH
Lifelines:
  Selected Poems
  1950–1999
Selves

JIM CARROLL
Fear of Dreaming:
  The Selected Poems
Living at the Movies
Void of Course

SU CHO
The Symmetry of Fish

RIO CORTEZ
Golden Ax

ALISON HAWTHORNE
DEMING
Genius Loci
Rope
Stairway to Heaven

CARL DENNIS
Another Reason
Callings
Earthborn
New and Selected Poems
  1974–2004
Night School
Practical Gods
Ranking the Wishes
Unknown Friends

DIANE DI PRIMA
Loba

STUART DISCHELL
Backwards Days
Dig Safe

STEPHEN DOBYNS
Velocities:
  New and Selected Poems
  1966–1992

EDWARD DORN
Way More West

HEID E. ERDRICH
Little Big Bully

ROGER FANNING
The Middle Ages

ADAM FOULDS
The Broken Word:
  An Epic Poem of the
  British Empire in Kenya,
  and the Mau Mau Uprising
  Against It

CARRIE FOUNTAIN
Burn Lake
Instant Winner
The Life

AMY GERSTLER
Dearest Creature
Ghost Girl
Index of Women
Medicine
Nerve Storm
Scattered at Sea

EUGENE GLORIA
Drivers at the Short-Time Motel
Hoodlum Birds
My Favorite Warlord
Sightseer in This Killing City

DEBORA GREGER
In Darwin's Room

TERRANCE HAYES
American Sonnets for
  My Past and Future Assassin
Hip Logic
How to Be Drawn
Lighthead
Wind in a Box

NATHAN HOKS
The Narrow Circle

ROBERT HUNTER
Sentinel and Other Poems

MARY KARR
Viper Rum

WILLIAM KECKLER
Sanskrit of the Body

JACK KEROUAC
Book of Blues
Book of Haikus
Book of Sketches

JOANNA KLINK
Circadian
Excerpts from a Secret
  Prophecy
The Nightfields
Raptus

JOANNE KYGER
As Ever: Selected Poems

ANN LAUTERBACH
Hum
If in Time: Selected Poems
  1975–2000
On a Stair
Or to Begin Again
Spell
Under the Sign

CORINNE LEE
Plenty
Pyx

PHILLIS LEVIN
May Day
Mercury
Mr. Memory & Other Poems

PATRICIA LOCKWOOD
Motherland Fatherland
  Homelandsexuals

WILLIAM LOGAN
Rift of Light

J. MICHAEL MARTINEZ
Museum of the Americas

ADRIAN MATEJKA
The Big Smoke
Map to the Stars
Mixology
Somebody Else Sold the World

MICHAEL MCCLURE
Huge Dreams: San Francisco
  and Beat Poems

ROSE MCLARNEY
Forage
Its Day Being Gone

DAVID MELTZER
David's Copy:
  The Selected Poems of
  David Meltzer

TERESA K. MILLER
Borderline Fortune

ROBERT MORGAN
Dark Energy
Terroir

CAROL MUSKE-DUKES
An Octave Above Thunder:
  New and Selected Poems
Red Trousseau
Blue Rose
Twin Cities

ALICE NOTLEY
Certain Magical Acts
Culture of One
The Descent of Alette
Disobedience
For the Ride
In the Pines
Mysteries of Small Houses

WILLIE PERDOMO
The Crazy Bunch
The Essential Hits of Shorty
  Bon Bon

DANIEL POPPICK
Fear of Description

LIA PURPURA
It Shouldn't Have Been
  Beautiful

LAWRENCE RAAB
The History of Forgetting

BARBARA RAS
The Last Skin
One Hidden Stuff

MICHAEL ROBBINS
Alien vs. Predator
The Second Sex
Walkman

PATTIANN ROGERS
Generations
Holy Heathen Rhapsody
Quickening Fields
Wayfare

SAM SAX
Madness

ROBYN SCHIFF
A Woman of Property

WILLIAM STOBB
Absentia
Nervous Systems

TRYFON TOLIDES
An Almost Pure Empty
  Walking

VINCENT TORO
Tertulia

PAUL TRAN
All the Flowers Kneeling

SARAH VAP
Viability

ANNE WALDMAN
Gossamurmur
Kill or Cure
Manatee/Humanity
Trickster Feminism

JAMES WELCH
Riding the Earthboy 40

PHILIP WHALEN
Overtime: Selected Poems

PHILLIP B. WILLIAMS
Mutiny

ROBERT WRIGLEY
Anatomy of Melancholy and
  Other Poems
Beautiful Country
Box
Earthly Meditations:
  New and Selected Poems
Lives of the Animals
Reign of Snakes
The True Account of Myself
  as a Bird

MARK YAKICH
The Importance of Peeling
  Potatoes in Ukraine
Spiritual Exercises
Unrelated Individuals Forming
  a Group Waiting to Cross